TAN/cm

My
SMARTPHONE
and other digital accessories

FRANKLIN WATTS

LONDON•SYDNEY

First published in 2014 by
Franklin Watts
338 Euston Road
London
NW1 3BH

Franklin Watts Australia
Level 17/207 Kent Street
Sydney
NSW 2000

HB ISBN 978 1 4451 3279 2
Library ebook ISBN 978 1 4451 3281 5

A CIP catalogue record for this book is
available from the British Library.

Series Editor: Julia Bird
Packaged by: Q2A Media

Picture credits:
Cover: Photobuay, Darrin Henry, Umberto Shtanzman, Jeka, Barone Firenze, Chaoss, AdrianNunez, Queezz/
Shutterstock. Back Cover: NorGal/Shutterstock. Title Page: (T) Solarseven/Shutterstock; (B) Peshkova/Shutterstock.
Imprint Page: Oleksiy Mark/Shutterstock. P4: Nmedia/Shutterstock; P5: Ekler/Shutterstock; P6: Bakalusha/
Shutterstock; P7(T): Maxx Studio/Shutterstock; P7(B): Tong chuwit/Shutterstock; P8: Fairphone; P9: Bloomberg/
Contributer/Getty Images; P10: Goodluz/Shutterstock; P11(L): TongChuwit/Shutterstock; P11(R): E+/Getty Images;
P12(T): Nager-IT; P12(B): Lucas Oleniuk/Zuma Press/Corbis; P13(B): Erni/Shutterstock; P13(TL): Q2A Media;
P13(TR): Ecovative Design; P14(B): Darrin Henry/Shutterstock; P15: BartlomiejMagierowski/Shutterstock; P16(C):
Dmitry Kalinovsky/Shutterstock; P16(B): BartlomiejMagierowski/Shutterstock; P17: Nokia; P18(TL): David Pearson/
Alamy; P18(B): Derek Latta/Shutterstock; P19: Gilles Paire/Shutterstock; P20(Bgrnd): MartinMaritz/Shutterstock;
P20(B): Wlad74/Shutterstock; P21(T): Ventus Innovative Products; P21(BL): TongChuwit/Shutterstock; P21(BR):
Berlin Boombox; P22(T): Canadapanda/Shutterstock; P22(B): Christian Bertrand/Shutterstock; P23: Neveshkin
Nikolay/Shutterstock; P24(Bgrnd): Olivier Asselin/Alamy; P24(TR): TongChuwit/Shutterstock; P24(BR): Eliza
Grinnell/Harvard Seas; P25: Wiklander/Shutterstock; P26: Waldru/Shutterstock; P27(B): Imaginechina/Corbis;
P27(T): TongChuwit/Shutterstock; P28: Stringer Shanghai/Reuters; P29(TR): Worldreader; P29(BL): PC Plus
Magazine/Getty; P29(BR): TongChuwit/Shutterstock; P30–31: Saicle/Shutterstock; P31(L): Oleksiy Mark/
Shutterstock; P31(C): Shutterstock; P31(R): Barone Firenze/Shutterstock.
Index Page: Sergey Nivens/Shutterstock.
Illustration: All-free-downloads.com (P10–11, 14, 18, 19, 21, 22–23).

Printed in Malaysia

Franklin Watts is a division of
Hachette Children's Books,
an Hachette UK company.
www.hachette.co.uk

Contents

Words in **bold** can be found in the glossary on pages 30–31.

Smart trade

The latest smart devices make huge profits for the big electronics companies. However, the miners and factory workers who help produce these devices often work in unsafe conditions and are badly paid. Fair trade schemes are working together to try and stop this happening.

Everyone wants to use the latest laptops, smartphones and tablets.

What are fair trade schemes?

The demand for electronic smart devices is growing all the time. Making these devices can provide much-needed work for many people, especially those in developing countries. Fair trade schemes are ways of making sure that these workers are paid a fair price for what they do. The schemes also aim to build strong communities that are able to care for themselves and their environment. Pressure from customers and environmental organisations has created fair trade schemes that are slowly working to improve people's lives.

Explore the issues

This book explains where our electronic devices come from and explores some of the problems associated with making them, from poor or dangerous working conditions for workers, to the environmental damage that manufacturing them can cause. It looks at some solutions already in place, explains why fair trade is vital and discusses what you can do to help.

Labelling gadgets

Food can be labelled to show its origins, but with digital devices it is more difficult. Each device may contain hundreds of parts that are produced and manufactured in many different countries. Because of this, it can be hard to keep track of where every piece is made and under what conditions. Today, more electronics companies are starting to take responsibility for their **supply chain** as a result of increased pressure from customers.

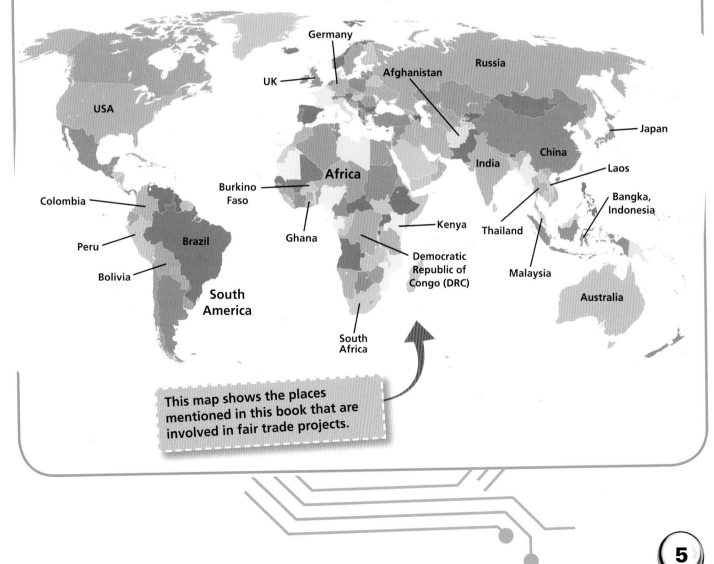

This map shows the places mentioned in this book that are involved in fair trade projects.

Smartphones

By 2015, it is estimated there will be more smartphones in the world than people! China is the biggest market for smartphones – 30 million were sold in August 2012 alone. India and the USA are close behind. Smartphones are expensive, but most people still expect to upgrade their model every 18 months or so.

What is in a smartphone?

There are hundreds of different parts to a smartphone, each made from a wide range of materials, including copper in the wires, gold in the circuit boards and over 40 different chemical elements. All phones contain around two grammes of tin, which is used to make the **solder** that holds the parts together. The electronics industry uses almost half of all the tin mined today.

Phones are often seen as disposable. It is estimated that in 2012 in the USA alone 140 million smart and mobile phones ended up in landfill.

Re-use, recycle

A discarded mobile or smartphone takes 1,000 years to break down. To be eco-friendly, it's best to keep the phone you already have, and replace parts if they go wrong. Or if you really want to get rid of your old smartphone, try recycling it – find out about a scheme near you.

Where are smartphones made?

Smartphones travel a long way to reach their customers and many different countries are involved in their production and assembly. For example, the Apple iPhone is designed in North America, while the **microchip** controlling the phone's graphics is designed by Imagination Technologies in the UK. The 'gyroscope' that lets you use a phone lengthways or sideways comes from a French-Italian company.

The metals that are used to make an iPhone's components may have been mined in Africa, China or Indonesia. Finally, the phones are most often assembled in an Asian factory. Eighty-five per cent of iPhone 5s were put together in China.

Tin mine trouble

Tin is used in most electronic devices, including smartphones. It is dug out of rocks made of heavy clay or sifted through huge puddles of dirty, muddy water. Mining tin is hard, heavy and dangerous work. Many tin mines in countries such as Africa and China are not properly equipped or supervised; health and safety standards are poor or don't exist. Tin miners are expected to work long hours for very little pay. Breathing in tin dust can cause all sorts of illnesses, from sore eyes and skin problems to liver and brain damage.

Environmental damage

Poor practice in the mines can devastate the local environment. Dangerous chemicals can get into the water system and poison the water people drink. **Toxins** can also get into the seas and kill the fish that provide food for local people, as well as destroying healthy coral reefs.

Good buy!

In the eastern Democratic Republic of Congo (DRC), armed **militia** control the tin mines, sometimes forcing miners to work at gunpoint and terrorising local villagers, which is why the tin produced here is known as 'conflict tin'. The electronics company, Fairphone, sources its tin from the Conflict-Free Tin Initiative in the DRC, where the mines are carefully monitored and miners are paid a fair price for the tin they produce. Local **co-operatives** buy safety equipment, such as helmets and boots, and make sure the mineshafts are stable. A tracking system means producers can see that their tin has come from a responsibly managed mine.

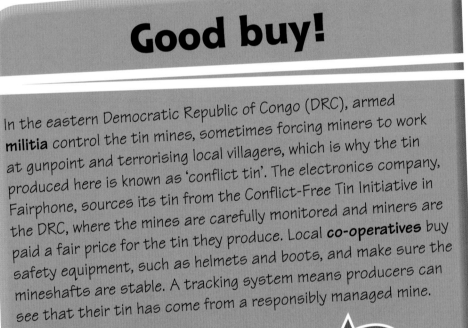

The Fairphone uses 'conflict-free' tin. The phone comes apart easily, so parts can be recycled and replaced.

Case study: Bangka Island tin mines, Indonesia

The tin mines on Bangka Island are dangerous places to work – on average in 2011 one miner died every week due to work-related accidents or illness. Some are buried alive when there is a mud slide. But the pay is good: up to £5 a day. This money helps the local people to pay for things they could not otherwise afford, such as sending their children to school.

Buried alive

In 2012, Suge, a miner, was buried in a landslide at a tin mine, but he was one of the lucky ones – he was dug out alive and survived with just a broken arm and leg. His boss promised to pay him some compensation and said that he could have his job back when he was better. But in most mines, there would be no compensation and no job.

Poor practice in the mines is destroying forests, beaches and farms, and ruining Bangka's tourist trade. While tin still makes money for local people today, the island's future does not look so bright.

A mine worker at a Bangka Island tin mine. Every year over 900,000 tonnes of tin are extracted from mines in Indonesia.

Laptops

Laptops are more convenient and portable than a desktop computer and use around 25 per cent less energy. But do you know what's inside your laptop?

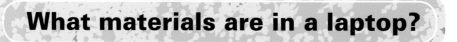

What materials are in a laptop?

Up to 50 per cent of your laptop is made up of as many as 20 different types of metal, including lead, copper and mercury. Coltan is also an essential ingredient – it is a metallic **ore** that can hold a very high electrical charge and stops a laptop from over-heating.

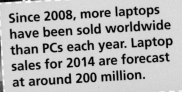

Since 2008, more laptops have been sold worldwide than PCs each year. Laptop sales for 2014 are forecast at around 200 million.

What are microchips made of?

There are thousands of parts inside a laptop, including a microchip. This tiny piece goes through hundreds of stages of manufacture, including treatment with toxic chemicals and gases so that it can conduct electricity. Microchips are made from silica, which comes from a type of sand that may have been mined in Brazil, refined in Germany, converted to **polysilicon** in Japan, turned into super-thin plate in the USA and made into microchips in Malaysia. Finally, the chips often find their way onto a **circuit board** in China.

Re-use, recycle

In some countries, **e-waste** is burnt and dangerous smoke fills the surrounding air. To help stop this, you can recycle your laptop through a local council scheme. Some online companies will collect unwanted computers and recycle them for charity. Check out your local recycling options.

Case study: Coltan mine, Democratic Republic of Congo, Africa

Some people call coltan 'black gold', because it has brought wealth to a very poor region of Africa. However, most miners have no idea where their coltan will end up, or how much it is really worth. In some mines, workers earn up to £30 a week from coltan. In others, young children, such as 10-year-old Eudes, have been forced to give up school and work in the mine instead, for just £1 per day. The work is hard and dull. Eudes has to scrabble in the mud, rinsing earth from the mineral deposits he finds. He doesn't have any safety equipment.

Eudes also fears that soldiers, who control the mine, will come and take his money, or his coltan, to buy weapons.

Good buy!

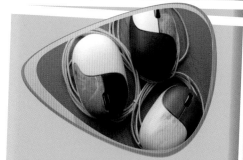

No laptops can yet claim to be 100 per cent fair trade, but a German company called Nager-IT has been working to produce a fair trade mouse. It uses components from mines where there is no forced overtime, no child labour, health protection, fair wages and recognition of human rights.

It can take Eudes several days to mine just a few grams of coltan.

Conflict-free coltan

Coltan comes from mines in the Democratic Republic of Congo among other countries. A terrible civil war in the DRC ended in 2003, but rebel soldiers are still active and they fight and kill to take control of the precious coltan mines. As a result, coltan has become known as a 'conflict mineral'. The Solutions for Hope project was set up in 2011 by the US company Motorola Solutions. Its aim is to make sure that conflict-free mines sell their coltan directly to a monitored co-operative. The co-operative then prepares the laptop components for Motorola. That way Motorola knows where the tin comes from and can label it 'conflict-free'.

Environment matters

Polystyrene packaging is made from oil, which is hard to recycle and takes years to break down; it also pollutes our oceans. Dell, a computer manufacturer, now sells its laptops in protective packaging made from **sustainable** bamboo.

This Dell server is protected by compostable packaging made from crop waste that is held together by a mushroom root.

The DRC's gorilla population has fallen by 90 per cent and they are now seriously endangered.

Endangered gorillas

Huge areas of rainforest in the DRC have been cleared to make way for coltan mines. People moving to find work in the mines chop down trees for fuel, and eat bushmeat, such as gorillas. Kemet, the world's largest producer of coltan used in laptops, has asked its supply chains to make sure that the coltan they supply is 'conflict-free'. In the US, campaigns encourage the recycling of electronic waste to provide an alternative source of coltan. Both these schemes may help to protect the DRC gorillas.

Digital cameras

The first photograph was developed in 1827, and since then billions of photographs have been taken. Every day at least 30 million photos are uploaded to Facebook.

62mm 1:1.4

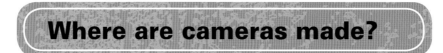

Where are cameras made?

A camera can contain over 180 parts. **Raw materials** are shipped from around the world to the factories where the cameras are put together. Camera companies often have their products assembled in south-east Asian countries, such as Thailand, China and Laos, where lower wages help to keep the price down.

Selfies are used for Facebook, blogs and to share with friends.

How is the lens made?

Special optical glass starts off as a powder made up of hundreds of raw materials, such as plastic, rubber and steel. The powder is heated, melted, cut and shaped to make the lens. Both sides of the lens go through several stages of polishing. Finally, a thin film is applied to the finished lens to stop reflection.

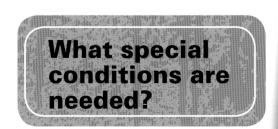

What special conditions are needed?

Conditions in the camera factories have to be just right. The lens, for example, needs to be polished, washed and inspected many times. The factory has 'clean rooms' where all workers wear masks, gloves and special protective clothing. One tiny speck of dust can affect how well the lens works.

This factory worker wears special clothing to prevent dust damaging the lens of the CCTV camera he is making.

Difficult market for cameras

Cameras take time to produce and can be expensive to make, yet **consumers** expect high-quality cameras at cheap prices. Today, digital cameras are competing with smartphones that have built-in cameras, so manufacturers have to keep costs down to make their product more appealing.

Case study: Tianjin camera factory, China

Compared to many factories in the area, Tianjin camera factory offers good working conditions.

Zhao is 19 and works up to 12-hour shifts as a camera inspector. She doesn't have to travel far to get to work as she lives in a dormitory at the factory. This is normal practice in China, and the dorms in Tianjin are clean and air-conditioned. With overtime, Zhao can earn between £193 and £386 a month, which is more than neighbouring factories pay.

Tianjin factory's 50,000 employees assemble mobile phones, TVs, CCTV cameras and digital cameras. Assembly line workers put together 200–300 camera lenses each day.

Re-use, recycle

Never throw an old camera in the bin. Toxins inside it are dangerous for the environment. For older digital cameras, spare parts can be hard to come by, so try taking it back to a photography shop instead. Alternatively, you could help a charity by donating your old camera to them.

Some specialist camera shops are happy to buy old cameras if they are collectable.

China Labour Watch is a **not-for-profit organisation** that works with others to assess the conditions in China's digital camera factories. It has reported that in some factories, workers were not paid for their overtime, that they were forced to work long hours without a break, and got into serious trouble if they did not work fast enough. In most factories there was no one to complain to, and workers were not allowed to join a **union**.

As a result of the report, one manufacturer, Samsung, agreed to set up a plan to improve working conditions. They agreed to ensure that the factories they used to create the parts for their electronic goods followed local labour laws, as well as Samsung's own employment policies.

Good buy!

Nokia was voted the most sustainable company in the world in 2010 by the independent environmental organisation Greenpeace, in its Green Electronics Guide. Nokia says it aims to track supply chains and source materials used in its products ethically. Nokia builds its factories close to where its products will be sold and continues to use a high percentage of **renewable energy** as caring for the environment is still a high priority.

Nokia was the first company to produce a phone with a built-in camera.

Environment Matters

Digital cameras guzzle batteries like no other device. Batteries are bad for the environment. They contain dangerous chemicals that can contaminate the ground, the water systems and the air if they are not disposed of properly. If you buy a new camera, make sure it has rechargeable batteries.

MP3 players and iPods

Portable music players, such as MP3 players and iPods, were developed so that whole music collections could be stored on this one tiny device.

What is an MP3 player made of?

As with all electronic devices, an MP3 player is made from a wide range of materials, including silicon, liquid crystals, plastic and precious metals, which can include gold, silver and platinum.

Portable music players have changed the way we listen to music.

Workers in an open-pit mine in Burkino Faso, West Africa. The best way to mine gold is to create an underground shaft, but this is expensive and can take a long time.

Where does the gold come from?

Gold is used in MP3 players to make electric switches and connect wires. Around the world, there are several hundred gold mines, but just 20 countries produce three quarters of the world's gold. In 2013, the top producers were China, Australia and the USA. Gold is difficult to find and it takes about 3,000 tonnes of rock to produce just 10–15 kg of gold. Environmental group Friends of the Earth claim that you could find more gold in a tonne of mobile phones than in a tonne of rock from a gold mine.

Dirty gold mining

Many gold mines around the world are open-pit mines. This means that explosives are used to blast the rock to reach the gold. This is a dirty gold mining practice that destroys huge areas of the environment.

Another dirty gold mining practice is heap leaching. Rocks are heaped up and sprayed with a deadly chemical called cyanide, which sticks to the gold. The cyanide soaks into the ground, where it pollutes the soil and poisons the water supply. Some mines use a liquid metal called mercury to find gold. Mercury fumes are deadly for wildlife and humans, and can damage the liver, brains and lungs.

Case study: Dreifontein Mine, South Africa

In September 2013, 80,000 gold miners at Dreifontein went on strike for better wages, even though it meant they'd earn no money.

Albertina, a miner, starts work at 3.45 in the morning, and has to work deep under the ground, where the heat is unbearable. Her shift lasts eight hours and during that time, miners are bent double in the cramped tunnels. However, conditions have improved – there are fewer accidents than there used to be, the workers get breaks for fresh air, and there are fans to protect them from the heat. Albertina takes home around £300 per month in wages, which is not enough to feed her family.

Struggling industry

Strikes are continuing at South Africa's gold mines, and the gold industry is struggling. The lack of production is putting pressure on the economy. It is estimated that each strike day costs the country £22 million. Mining companies say they cannot afford to pay the wages the miners are demanding.

The 'headgear' at the top of the gold mineshaft hauls up minerals from deep underground.

Gold ore: about 40 per cent of the gold ore mined in the world comes from South Africa.

Fairtrade gold

Fairtrade gold was launched in 2011 in Peru, Bolivia and Colombia. Fairtrade miners respect their environment and follow safe working practices. They are paid a fair, minimum price for their gold, and given $2,000 (£1,188) per kilogram extra for local improvement projects on top of their pay. In the Sotrami community, in Peru, after less than two years of mining Fairtrade gold, the community was able to open up a grocery shop, improve the local health and dental care services and clean up the water supply.

Good buy!

Instead of having a plug, the Spin Eco media player has a handle so you can wind it up. One minute of winding provides 45 minutes of sound – and vision. Once it's fully charged, this device will keep playing for 55 hours. You can also use it to view photos and videos, store up to 2,000 tunes and even recharge your phone.

Once you've finished with it, the Spin Eco media player can be recycled.

Re-use, recycle

When it comes to using your iphone, ipod or MP3 with speakers, slotting it into a Berlin Boombox is a brilliant eco-option. The Boombox comes in a do-it-yourself cardboard pack that turns into an eco-speaker, with just a few electronic parts.

This brown Boombox is 100 per cent recyclable.

Games consoles – Xbox

The first home video game that could be connected to a television was launched in 1972. Today, millions of homes worldwide have a games console.

When the new Xbox One was launched in 13 countries, in 2013, one million units were sold in just 24 hours.

What is in a games console?

Among the many components of an Xbox games console is a **multi-core processor**, which holds several processors on one chip. These control the functions of the console, such as the graphics and the sound. In 2008, Greenpeace took apart a number of games consoles from different manufacturers, and discovered there were several toxic chemicals inside. PVC is used to coat cables and wires, while other chemicals are used to stop the gadget catching fire.

Are these chemicals dangerous?

Children's toys are checked for dangerous ingredients, but computers and games consoles are not classed as toys. If they were, they would be banned from shops in some parts of the world. The greatest dangers, however, are probably from the chemical fumes the workers who assemble the technology are exposed to. Good **ventilation** and protection from the fumes is essential to keep workers healthy.

A 2008 MakeITFair report showed that some workers in games console factories in China, particularly those in the soldering sections, regularly felt sick after inhaling toxic fumes and some workers needed to be hospitalised, even though they were wearing masks and ventilation was up to standard.

Future damage

If you don't dispose of your console carefully, the chemicals inside could become part of the growing mountain of e-waste.

Although e-waste should now be 100 per cent recyclable, some still finds its way to countries such as China, India and Russia, where fires used to burn the old electronic equipment create toxic fumes. Children living in these areas have been found to have higher levels of toxins in their blood.

Most consoles use up huge amounts of energy. 3-D games require plenty of electrical power as does watching a video through your console, and using the console with your TV screen.

Case study: e-waste mountains, Ghana, Africa

The dumping of e-waste is illegal, but container ships still arrive in the port of Accra, Ghana's capital city, full of so-called 'second hand' electronics. Most of these old devices are useless, and end up dumped at scrap markets. Families often send their children to Accra to work on the scrap markets. Here, children aged as young as eight spend 12 hours a day sifting through the piles of electronic waste looking for copper and aluminium they can sell for cash. They use their bare hands as they burn off the plastic from the wires to get to the metal, creating hazardous, black toxic fumes.

Fires like this one burn all day to destroy old electronic devices. The toxic fumes can cause breathing disorders and damage workers' immune systems.

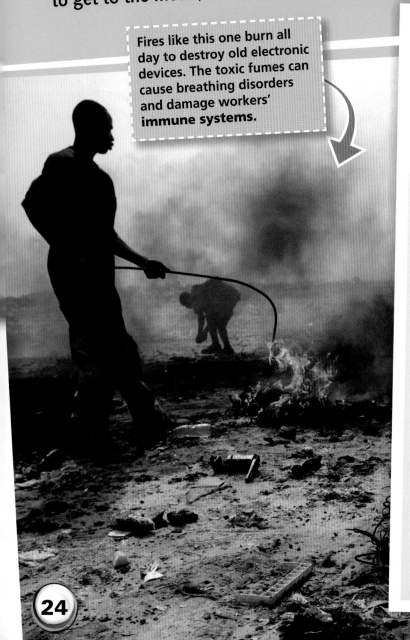

Re-use, recycle

After reading about the e-waste problems in Ghana, US engineering student Rachel Field came up with a simple idea she calls the 'Bicyclean'. She fitted an ordinary bicycle with a 'grinding wheel' that would break up electronic waste without the need for heat. The waste is caught in a box, along with any harmful dust, and all materials are recycled – including any plastic.

Taking responsibility

Greenpeace highlighted the problem of e-waste in India in 2005. Since then, Indian electronics producers have been encouraged to ban toxic substances from their products. In 2011, new laws were introduced to make all companies take responsibility for goods they have produced when they reach the end of their life.

A new scheme, sponsored by computer giant Dell, has helped 27 women in Nairobi, Kenya, who once collected waste from scrap heaps. The women have been trained and given loans so they can buy and sort e-waste to resell at a brand-new e-waste recycling centre. The workers are given a fair price for their work, and no longer have to put their health at risk.

Environment Matters

Your computer monitor accounts for about one third of the electricity that your computer uses. Switch off your computer whenever you are away from your desk, or at least make sure it is in 'sleep' mode, and turn off screensavers.

By 2020, electronic companies will have recycled around 900 million kg of electronic devices at the Nairobi e-waste centre.

Tablets and e-readers

The first e-reader was launched in 1998 and many models quickly followed. Sales in 2011 soared to 27.7 million... but then the tablet took over, with around 250 million sales in 2013!

What is in your tablet?

All today's tabets contain **rare earth minerals**. There are 17 different types of 'rare earths', and they come in a powdered form. They are expensive, but without them your tablet probably would not exist. Rare earth minerals are in the magnets that keep your device small and make it work fast, the colours behind your screen, the touchscreen element and even the polish that makes your tablet shine.

A tablet lets you read a book, watch a movie, talk to a friend on Skype... everything with just one device.

Where do rare earths come from?

Rare earths can be found all over the world, but they are difficult to **excavate**. China is the main producer of rare earths, but it has cut back on sales to the rest of the world because of environmental concerns. (see page 28). Now other countries are scrambling to find new supplies or alternative materials. Excavations are underway in Bolivia and Afghanistan.

Mining hazards

Extracting and processing rare earths can damage the environment if it is not done properly. Rare earths are often found with **radio-active** elements and if these are not monitored and controlled, they can enter the ground, water systems and the air.

Re-use, recycle

Japan has no rare earth resources of its own, but is aiming to produce 300,000 tonnes of rare earth metals by recycling components from its e-waste mountain.

A rare earth mine in south-west China. China's rare earth industry makes up 97 per cent of the world's rare mineral trade.

Case study: Baotou, Inner Mongolia, China

Li Guirong was born in a village near Baotou in the 1940s. He remembers the time when there were fields full of fruit and vegetables in the area. Gradually, pollution from local industries caused the crops to die back, until they did not grow at all. Today, a dam of filthy water covers 10 km of land. There is no life in the water. Instead it is polluted with waste from rare earth processing and from other factories in the area. The chemicals that are used to extract rare earth minerals and radioactive material can cause various types of cancer if they get into the body. Water from the dam has already polluted the **ground water** in the area and is moving towards the Yellow River, which provides drinking water for most of Northern China.

Ghost village

Ten years ago, 2,000 people lived in Li's village. Today, so many people have moved away there are just 300 people left. The Chinese government is at last taking notice of the environmental problems that rare earth mining is causing. Billions of dollars are now being spent in an attempt to clean up the environment, and rare earth exports have been limited.

Labourers at Baotou, China's largest rare earth mine. China produces 95 per cent of the world's rare earths.

Getting better?

Many different organisations monitor the ethical and environmental performance of many devices we use. They assess the sourcing of the device's materials, treatment of workers, the environmental impact of the device and its energy consumption. By making this information available, they make customers aware of where and how their electronic devices are produced, which in turn puts pressure on companies to increase and improve their environmental and fair trade practices. Using these criteria, the Ethical Consumer magazine examined a range of tablets.

The winner, the Archos Internet tablet, scored just ten points out of a possible 20. There is still a long way to go but at least people are thinking of ways to improve the manufacture of our electronic devices.

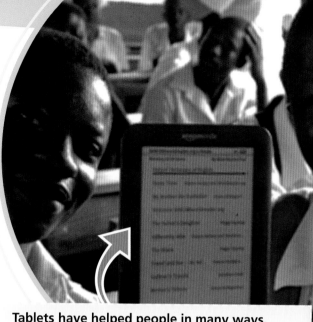

Tablets have helped people in many ways. Organisations such as **Worldreader** are helping to improve literacy skills in Africa by replacing out-of-date school books with e-readers.

Re-use, recycle

The Ellen MacArthur Foundation thinks there is a better way to buy. Their plan is for a 'circular economy' where products are designed so they will not produce waste and do not use hazardous chemicals, but do use renewable energy. Instead of buying a new e-reader, for example, you would 'rent' it, and because it would be easy to take apart, you could upgrade and change it whenever you wanted. Then, at the end of its working life, it would go back to the rental company for easy recycling.

The Archos Internet tablet

Glossary

circuit board A piece of electrical equipment that slots into a computer to make it work faster and better

compostable A material that will break down or rot easily and quickly

consumers People who buy or use goods and services for personal use

co-operatives When people or groups work together so that everyone benefits

e-waste (or electronic waste) All discarded electronic devices and equipment

excavate To dig out or remove ores or coal etc., from the earth

ground water Water that is in the ground, just beneath the surface

human rights Basic rights, such as being safe, free and able to look after yourself and your family

immune system The system of organs, tissues and cells that protect the body from infection

landfill Deep, lined pits used to bury waste

manufacture To make, usually in a factory

microchip A tiny piece of silicon able to hold millions of circuits

militia Rebel soldiers who are not supported by a government

multi-core processor Where several processors are combined onto one chip, so work is divided between the various processors, increasing the computing possibilities and saving energy at the same time

not-for-profit organisation A company that operates without a view to making money

ore Rock containing a combination of minerals including metals, such as iron or gold, that occurs naturally in the ground or in rocks and that are mined for profit

polysilicon A material made up of many silicon crystals. Silicon is a substance that is found naturally in the earth

poor practice Behaviour or ways of working or treating workers that are below acceptable standards

radio active Rays or particles that come from nuclear waste that can cause illness or death

rare earth minerals A collection of 17 minerals found naturally in the ground that are used in electronic devices

raw materials Basic materials, such as coal and wood, before they are manufactured

renewable energy A source of energy that occurs naturally, such as solar (sun) energy, wave or wind energy

solder To join two metals together with heat

supply chain The journey a product goes through, from sourcing of materials through to when the finished product reaches the customer

sustainable Something that can be kept going or maintained in the future without damaging the environment or its resources

toxins Dangerous substances that can poison and harm humans, animals and the environment

union An organisation of workers who join together to protect the rights and interests of its members

ventilation A way of keeping the air fresh by taking out stale or toxic air and replacing it with clean air

Websites

See some Greenpeace campaigns online: **www.greenpeace.org.uk/what-we-do**

Find out more about Friends of the Earth here: **www.foe.co.uk/what_we_do_index**

Here's a video that shows how and where smartphones are made: **www.youtube.com/watch?v=8EqXQ42QAaY&feature=youtu.be**

Find out about another new smartphone concept here: **www.phonebloks.com/en/goals**

Make IT Fair is a European organisation set up to tell young people around the world about what's happening in the electronics industry: **hwww.makeitfair.org/en**

If you want to dispose of old mobile phones responsibly (any profit made from your phones goes to a charity of your choice) visit this website: **www.shpforcharity.co.uk/**

This is how a laptop is made: **www.youtube.com/watch?v=5QC_QShyus0**

See the steps silicon goes through to make a computer chip: **www.intel.com/content/www/us/en/history/museum-making-silicon.html**

Here's the supply chain for Nager-IT's mouse – you won't believe it! **www.nager-it.de/static/pdf/en_lieferkette.pdf**

Find out more about the Berlin Boombox here: **www.berlinboombox.com**

Admire some fairtrade gold jewellery, and see where it comes from: **www.credjewellery.com/**

This is what happens to some of our e-waste: **www.youtube.com/watch?v=pr1zQrXM_7s**

Here's the story of Bicyclean – an amazingly simple invention to help solve the problem of e-waste: **www.seas.harvard.edu/news/2013/06/designing-cleaner-future**

Here is one of Worldreader's projects that bring e-readers to African schools: **www.worldreader.org/what-we-do/our-projects/south-africa/**

Find out more about rare earth metals in this video: **www.bbc.co.uk/news/world-asia-pacific-13777439**

Index